Create and Share | Thinking Digitally

Taking Digital Notes

By Amber Lovett

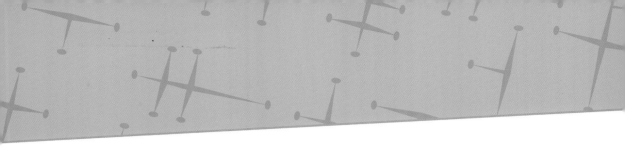

 CHERRY LAKE PRESS

Published in the United States of America by Cherry Lake Publishing Group
Ann Arbor, Michigan
www.cherrylakepublishing.com

Series Adviser: Kristin Fontichiaro
Reading Adviser: Marla Conn, MS, Ed., Literacy specialist, Read-Ability, Inc.
Book Designer: Felicia Macheske
Character Illustrator: Rachael McLean

Photo Credits: © bernatets photo/Shutterstock.com, 5; © Sakura Image Inc/Shutterstock.com, 11; © Chayanin Wongpracha/
Shutterstock.com, 13; © Monkey Business Images/Shutterstock.com, 17; © ilkercelik/Shutterstock.com, 21

Graphics Credits Throughout: © the simple surface/Shutterstock.com; © Diana Rich/Shutterstock.com; © lemony/
Shutterstock.com; © CojoMoxon/Shutterstock.com; © IreneArt/Shutterstock.com; © Artefficient/Shutterstock.com; © Marie
Nimrichterova/Shutterstock.com; © Svetolk/Shutterstock.com; © EV-DA/Shutterstock.com; © briddy/Shutterstock.com;
© Mix3r/Shutterstock.com

Cherry Lake Press is an imprint of Cherry Lake Publishing Group.

Library of Congress Cataloging-in-Publication Data

Names: Lovett, Amber, author. | McLean, Rachael, illustrator.
Title: Taking digital notes by Amber Lovett ; illustrated by Rachael McLean.
Description: Ann Arbor, Michigan : Cherry Lake Publishing, 2020.
| Series: Create and share: thinking digitally | Includes bibliographical
references and index. | Audience: Grades 2-3
Identifiers: LCCN 2020006973 (print) | LCCN 2020006974 (ebook)
| ISBN 9781534168732 (hardcover) | ISBN 9781534170414 (paperback)
| ISBN 9781534172258 (pdf) | ISBN 9781534174092 (ebook)
Subjects: LCSH: Note-taking—Juvenile literature.
Classification: LCC LB2395.25 .L68 2020 (print) | LCC LB2395.25 (ebook) |
 DDC 371.30281—dc23
LC record available at https://lccn.loc.gov/2020006973
LC ebook record available at https://lccn.loc.gov/2020006974

Cherry Lake Publishing Group would like to acknowledge the work of the Partnership for 21st Century Learning, a Network
of Battelle for Kids. Please visit *http://www.battelleforkids.org/networks/p21* for more information.

Printed in the United States of America
Corporate Graphics

Table of
CONTENTS

CHAPTER ONE

Why Take Notes?

Imagine you just learned that the Earth is 238,855 miles (384,400 kilometers) away from the Moon. That's so far! When you get home, you want to tell your parents what you learned. But wait, how many miles was it again? You can't remember. One way to make sure you remember important things is to write them down. This is called taking notes.

There are a lot of great reasons to take notes. If you forget something, notes can help. Reading notes before a test can help you study. Writing notes helps our brains soak up new information.

Taking notes in class will help you remember what you learned.

Are you ready to start taking notes? First, you need to decide how. You might have taken notes in class using a pencil and paper. But there are other ways to take notes. Many people like to take digital notes. These are notes taken using a computer, tablet, or smartphone. If you take notes on the computer, you might use a **keyboard**. Tablets and phones also have **apps** that you can use to take notes.

There are different ways to take notes in an app. You can take audio notes. Voice notes are recordings of your voice. Some apps listen to you speak and type what you say. You can write or draw in some note apps using a **stylus** or your finger.

You can take notes
on a phone or tablet.

Decide How to Take Notes

Not sure how to take notes? Ask an adult to help you download an app that will let you take notes by speaking, typing, and drawing.

1. Find a book or video you want to take notes on.
2. Try taking notes three different ways:
   - Type your notes using a keyboard.
   - Write your notes with your finger on the screen.
   - Take a voice note. Record your voice and watch your notes turn into words on the screen.
3. Read over your notes and decide how you like to take notes.

AudioNote and Otter Voice let you speak your notes. Apps like this listen to you talk and turn what you say into written notes. If you'd like to write your notes using your finger, try Squid. Some apps like Google keep, Evernote, Notability, and Apple Notes let you speak, type, and draw your notes!

CHAPTER TWO

Writing Notes

Notes help you remember. But sometimes it's hard to know what to write down. Think about how many words you hear in a day. It would be impossible to write *everything* down!

You don't have to write down all the words you hear or read. Notes don't need to be in full sentences. Only write down important words and the **main ideas**. Make sure your notes are simple and clear.

Think of some questions you want to answer before you start your notes. Write your questions down first, and then write the answers next to them. Use the words *who, what, where, when,* and *why* to start your questions. For example, imagine you are going to take notes on clouds. You write down "clouds" at the top of your paper. You want to know:

- **Who** are the scientists who study clouds?
- **What** are clouds made of?
- **Where** do clouds come from?
- **When** do you see the most clouds?
- **Why** do clouds form?

The answers to these questions are all **facts** about clouds. Answering questions in your notes will help you learn important facts.

You can learn new words using notes too. If you hear a new word, write down the word and what it means. Writing down new **vocabulary** words will help you study and remember them. It's also important to write down names of important people and dates in your notes

If your teacher writes something on the board, you should probably write it in your notes.

cumulonimbus

stratus

Taking Short Notes

Notes should use as few words as possible. For example, if a book says, "Most mice eat seeds or grass," you might make a note that reads, "Food = seeds, grass." Writing just the important words in your notes saves you time! Try turning the following sentences into short notes.

1. The United States of America is made up of 50 individual states.
2. The basketball game will begin at 7:00 p.m.
3. The first working airplane was built and tested by brothers Orville and Wilbur Wright in 1903.

Write the date at the top of your notes so you know when you wrote them.

CHAPTER THREE

Improving Your Notes

How do your notes look? Are your notes just words on paper? You can use shapes and lines, pictures, and color to make your notes more useful.

Using Shapes and Lines

Drawing lines or other shapes in your notes helps **organize** information. Lines can help you separate different information. You can also draw a box or circle around information to make it stand out more. Shapes and lines make your notes easy to read.

Scientists draw pictures of plants and animals in their notes.

Using Pictures

Notes don't always have to be words. You can use pictures in your notes too. Ask an adult for help adding pictures from the internet to your notes. You can also draw your own pictures. When you use pictures and words together, your brain processes the same information in two different ways. This helps you remember the information even better!

Using Color

Another way to make your notes more useful is to add color. Try changing the color of your pen in your notes app. You can also **highlight** important words or ideas using a different color. Using color like this will help you focus on the most important parts of your notes.

SOME THINGS YOU SHOULD WRITE AT THE TOP OF YOUR NOTES:

- Overall topic of your notes
- Today's date
- Your name

The first two points help you organize your notes and easily refer back to them. Writing your name on top of your notes is especially important if they're on loose paper. If your notes are misplaced, people know to give them back to you!

Using Notes to Compare

You can use your notes to compare things. For this activity, pick two of your favorite characters from a book or movie.

1. Open your notes app. Use an app that lets you write or draw with your finger.

2. Draw a vertical line down the middle. Now you have two sections to write in.

3. Write one character's name in each section.

4. Think about how the characters are different or similar. For example, if one of your characters is funny, write "funny" under that character's name.

5. Keep going until you fill your page. What do the characters have in common? What traits make them unique?

Color can make your notes useful and fun to look at.

CHAPTER FOUR

Using Your Notes

You have learned a lot about writing notes! Now it's time to learn how to use them. Notes have little value if you don't use them. Notes help us study for a test or quiz. Rereading your notes helps refresh your memory.

It's a good idea to reread your notes the day after you write them. The information is still in your mind, and reading it again will help your brain remember more of it. If you take notes for a class, you should study your notes. Start rereading your notes at least one week before a test. Read a little bit every day. You will probably remember much more information than you would if you did not take notes.

When you take digital notes, make sure you save them. You might need to pick a title when you save your notes. Pick a title that is simple and clear. One idea is to use the date and topic of your notes as the title.

Try rereading your notes the next day.

Use your notes to stay organized and to keep track of your homework or chores, like vacuuming twice a week or watering the plants every other week. Your notes might even help you come up with a new idea for a project or a question to explore. How will you use your notes?

Studying Your Notes

There are many different ways to study notes. The more ways you study, the more you will remember!

- Explain your notes to someone else.
- Make flashcards from your notes.
- Rewrite your notes using fewer words.
- Highlight the important people, places, dates, and things.
- Write a practice quiz using your notes. Ask a friend to quiz you, or quiz them.
- Draw a picture of an important idea from your notes.
- Act out an idea from your notes.

Which ways did you try? What was your favorite way to study?

Keep all of your notes in one app or folder so you can find them.

GLOSSARY

apps (APS) computer programs that perform special functions

facts (FAKTS) things that are true

highlight (HYE-lite) to color over text with a see-through color

keyboard (KEE-bord) groups of keys made for typing

main ideas (MAYN eye-DEE-uhz) the most important thoughts or information

organize (OR-guh-nize) to put in order or arrange in a planned way

stylus (STYE-luhs) a pointed instrument used for writing on a screen

vocabulary (voh-KAB-yuh-ler-ee) a word or words that are explained or defined

For More
INFORMATION

BOOK

Minden, Cecilia, and Kate Roth. *Writing a Journal*. Ann Arbor, MI: Cherry Lake Publishing, 2020.

WEBSITES

Ducksters
https://www.ducksters.com/study.php
This site is full of study- and homework-help resources for science, math, history, and more.

Quizlet
https://quizlet.com
Make digital flashcards to study your notes.

INDEX

About the AUTHOR

Amber Lovett is a certified school librarian and teacher. She lives with her husband, Karan, in Portland, Oregon.